How to Play the Drum for Beginners

A Comprehensive Guide to Learning, Playing, and Becoming Proficient at the Instrument

© **Copyright 2023 - All rights reserved.**

The content contained within this book may not be reproduced, duplicated, or transmitted without direct written permission from the author or the publisher.

Under no circumstances will any blame or legal responsibility be held against the publisher, or author, for any damages, reparation, or monetary loss due to the information contained within this book, either directly or indirectly.

Legal Notice:

This book is copyright protected. It is only for personal use. You cannot amend, distribute, sell, use, quote, or paraphrase any part of the content within this book without the consent of the author or publisher.

Disclaimer Notice:

Please note the information contained within this document is for educational and entertainment purposes only. All effort has been executed to present accurate, up-to-date, reliable, and complete information. No warranties of any kind are declared or implied. Readers acknowledge that the author is not engaging in the rendering of legal, financial, medical, or professional advice. The content within this book has been derived from various sources. Please consult a licensed professional before attempting any techniques outlined in this book.

By reading this document, the reader agrees that under no circumstances is the author responsible for any losses, direct or indirect, that are incurred as a result of the use of the information contained within this document, including, but not limited to, errors, omissions, or inaccuracies.

Table of Contents

Introduction 1

Chapter 1: The Fundamentals of Drumming 2

Chapter 2: Different Types of Drums and Drumsticks 11

Chapter 3: Basic Techniques 25

Chapter 4: Rhythm and Timing 35

Chapter 5: Exploring Drum Beats and Fills 43

Chapter 6: Playing Along to Music 50

Chapter 7: Mastering Drum Rudiments 56

Chapter 8: Progressing with Your Drumming 64

Conclusion 72

References 74

Introduction

Welcome to this short but concise guide on learning how to play the drums. You may be asking yourself a few questions at this point, like "Can I learn to play the drums at home?" or "How do I learn to play the drums in a band?" This guide will help you to get started.

The hardest aspect, like anything in life, is making the decision to learn. The initial steps are always difficult, but once you get going, you'll discover the rest will come naturally. You've already taken the first step toward realizing your goal of learning how to play the drums and all there is to know about them by purchasing this book. Even if you've never played before, your desire to learn and improve as a drummer will serve as your driving force.

This guide is simple to follow and contains plenty of step-by-step instructions to help you. It's easy to read, and I guarantee you'll be playing drums like a pro by the end!

Chapter 1: The Fundamentals of Drumming

You may be wondering why you should learn to play the drums if you already play another instrument. It will be among the most crucial things you do to advance your musicianship in general. Learning to play the drums is one of the finest methods to improve your understanding of groove and rhythm regardless of what instrument you currently play.

Musical Benefits

The clear advantage of drumming is that it helps you become more adept at timing and rhythm. Even if this isn't the only benefit of learning, it's one of the better ones. If you have good timing and rhythm on one instrument, you'll have it on all of your instruments. This helps more than just you. Additionally, it helps any band you perform in, as the rhythm is the responsibility of all the band members, not just one.

Across the Genres

1. Drums are used in almost all musical genres. Source: https://unsplash.com/photos/person-playing-drums-MjIMc6uhwrE?utm_content=creditShareLink&utm_medium=referral&utm_source=unsplash

No musical instrument is confined to a specific genre because all instruments can be modified in technique and style to fit many other genres. The drums are instruments that stand out because they have been played throughout history in almost every age and culture and are used in almost all musical genres.

Regardless of the genre, you'll find that at the foundation are the drums, which also help maintain the tempo. Let's examine the main genres where drums are utilized.

Rock Music

Rock and roll, a new kind of music, was first developed in the 1940s and 1950s and repurposed vintage instruments in inventive ways. Drums and guitar took center stage as the saxophone, piano, and other instruments that had previously led music faded into the background.

Early in the 20th century, the first bass drum pedal, operated by foot, was introduced. This brought drum kits into use, and rock music became popular. A snare drum, bass drum, and possibly a tom-tom, as well as numerous hi-hats and cymbals, were initially the standard drum kit parts. This changed when drummers started designing their own setups as time passed.

In the 1960s, 1970s, and 1980s, players experimented with and increased the size of their kits. However, with the introduction of computer music and digital drums, traditional rock drummers have come under threat. Today's rock drummers often use a simple 4-piece kit instead of larger setups.

Jazz Music

Jazz and rock grew up together in many ways and share some similarities. However, in other ways, jazz is completely different. It is quite uncompromising in style and has always been linked to the concept of freedom. Jazz music education broadens your musical horizons and teaches you new techniques for playing other instruments while you're having a great time. Improvisation is a key component of jazz music, and it also fosters creativity.

Jazz drummers don't use drumsticks, which is the main distinction between jazz drumming and other musical genres. They prefer to use brushes, which are typically made of metal or plastic. These provide drummers the ability to play in ways that are not possible with drumsticks. When jazz was just starting out, it was frequently performed in small spaces like bars, and therefore, the brushes were originally utilized in the

1920s to help muffle the sound of a snare drum. The drummer creates an eerie sound by sweeping the brush across the drum. There are many different sorts of brushes, and each has a specific application.

Blues Music

An excellent way to convey your emotions is through music, and the blues is the most emotional musical genre there is. A drummer needs to be able to convey the longing and grief that are typically at its center. You can use as much force as you like when playing the snare drum in rock music, but not when playing blues. You must be constrained and in control instead.

Blues drummers typically use similar drum kits to rock drummers. The actual character of the percussion section, though, comes from the bass drum, which is typically played with a constant stream of quarter notes—again, with restraint.

Drums are simple in blues music and typically use a linear playing style. This means only one voice is used at a time. When playing the blues, you must keep things simple and play gently, despite how difficult it may be to resist the impulse to go all out on the drums.

Classical Music

The fact that drums are rarely used in classical music distinguishes it from other musical styles. Instead, there are numerous different players and instruments in the percussion department. The tambourine, timpani, cymbals, bass drum, triangle, and snare drum are some examples of these.

The fact that classical music is composed for the entire orchestra, even though percussion is still the backbone that binds it all together, is another significant difference. During the time of Haydn and Mozart, the string, woodwind, and brass sections received the bulk of the attention, with the percussion section just contributing a few accents.

As you can see, the drum is one of the more popular instruments, appearing in virtually every genre, be it soft classical, haunting blues, upbeat jazz, or modern rock.

How to Set and Accomplish Your Drumming Goals

Everyone knows that the key to success is setting and working toward goals. The same holds true for drumming lessons. But creating those objectives entails more than merely jotting them down. You can figure out how to get there after you are clear on your goals. This is how it's done.

1. Work out What You Want to Achieve

Consider what you want to accomplish carefully. Focus on the experiences and abilities you want to acquire as a drummer. What kind of drummer do you want to become? What specific drumming techniques are you hoping to pick up? You need to concentrate on this during your practice sessions, whatever it may be.

2. Make that Decision

Your subconscious mind becomes aware of your decision and recognizes that you are serious when you decide to accomplish anything. Things get moving after a decision is made. Don't expect it to be simple. Despite the obstacles you will encounter and the potential detours in your way, you are now determined to reach your objectives.

To be fair, if your goal is to be the world's best drummer, you must be prepared to fail. Learning the basic drum strokes or playing any musical chart is achievable and measurable.

3. Do It

This is where many fail. They have goals and plans but don't do anything about achieving them. The only way to succeed is to act. Motivation will come after. Do one thing every day toward your goals, and before you know it, you'll have succeeded.

4. Track and Measure

Tracking your goals is important. Your drum teacher must track your progress and give you more goals and you must do the same. It may seem hard to track things initially, but it will benefit you in time. You will be more focused and will progress much faster. You'll also have a sense of achievement because you will know exactly what you've done and what needs to be done.

5. Set Benchmarks

While big goals are important, smaller ones are equally so. Breaking a major objective down into smaller ones makes it much easier to accomplish; otherwise, you'll probably give up trying. To encourage you to achieve those objectives, you can even build up a reward system.

6. Adjust

When you have achieved your goals, take the time to look over your progress and adjust things to take into account changes in your preferences. Then, create some new goals and go for them. The more you do, the better you will be.

The Health Benefits

Drumming isn't just about banging a drum. It also offers plenty of health benefits:

1. Reduces Stress

In the US, stress affects more than forty million individuals, but the majority of them don't get help. The good news is that drumming can help relieve the symptoms of stress. It boosts your well-being and mood because drumming is a physical workout. Exercise burns calories and releases feel-good chemicals.

2. Relieves Depression

Drum circles are especially good for this because they involve getting together with friends to play the drums and dance. Communal drumming has been shown to relieve depression by removing negativity and allowing you to feel more pleasant feelings.

3. Reduces Blood Pressure

Again, drumming is physical, and it can help you lose weight, get your heart pumping, and is a great cardio workout. All this adds up to lower blood pressure, so try to build drumming into your daily fitness regimen.

4. Helps You Control Pain

Drumming can help you manage chronic pain since it diverts your attention from it. Instead, you put all of your attention into your drumming, which causes the release of endorphins, a painkiller.

5. It Burns Calories

Considering that drumming is a physical activity, you already know this. A normal session may burn up to 500 calories and involves full-body movement, making it a great way to exercise.

6. It Increases Your Brain Power

It takes a lot of practice to develop the coordination of your legs and arms when learning to play the drums. People who are right-handed rarely use their left hand much, and vice versa. Both halves of your brain are used when you learn to play the drums, and your brain works considerably harder to build up the non-dominant side of your body, strengthening the limbs and boosting your mental capacity.

7. It Boosts Your Confidence

Your confidence increases significantly when you learn a new skill, like drumming. You put in the hours and do the hard work to practice, making you feel more confident about yourself. Learn to get past the challenges of playing the drums, and you can face pretty much anything life throws your way.

8. Better Coordination

Drumming improves coordination since it forces you to utilize both arms and both legs simultaneously. Although at first it may seem difficult, you will see progress each week. And as your coordination improves, so do your drumming talents.

9. Better Social Life

You join a sizable community the moment you learn how to play the drums. You may learn from another player, take classes, or even attend local meetups. This ensures your social life improves, and an even better way to do this is to go to a drum circle. Once you feel confident, think about putting a band together. You'll quickly make new friends and broaden your social network.

10. It Makes You Happier

When you add the benefits of playing, you can see it adds up to a happier life. You'll quickly realize how much you enjoy attending a drum circle or a drum cardio class if you give it a try. It is simple to understand how drumming makes you joyful when you take into account the endorphins your body releases.

Chapter 2: Different Types of Drums and Drumsticks

There is a huge variety of drums in use today, each with a different size and distinctive sound. Before looking at the various varieties of drumsticks and the accessories you may need to consider acquiring, here is an overview of the major ones even if it's not possible to cover them all.

Let's start with the drums.

Drum Set Types

Let's start by looking at the more familiar drum sets:

Acoustic:

2. *Acoustic drums are the most common type of drum set. Source: Dejan Krsmanovic, CC BY 2.0 <https://creativecommons.org/licenses/by/2.0>, via Wikimedia Commons: https://commons.wikimedia.org/wiki/File:Acoustic_Drums_Kit_(29965183378).jpg*

This is the most common type, and they are typically made up of:

- **Snare Drum:** This is usually placed right in the middle. When the snare drum is played, it gives off a sound that is similar to cracking.

- **Bass Drum:** Used with a beater or kick pedal.

- **Floor Tom:** This is the second largest drum and gives off a booming, low sound that has a very deep tone.

- **Rack Top:** This has an open sound that resonates with a tone that is definitive.

These drum sets can also be grouped as follows:

- **Rock/Power:** Typically have three toms – 12-inch, 13-inch, and 16-inch – and a bass drum 22 x 18-inch. Snares can be different, but they're usually 5 ½ to 6 inches by 14. They have a deep tone and increased volume.
- **Fusion:** These often have three toms – 10-inch, 12-inch, and 14-inch and a 20 or 22-inch by 18-inch bass. The sound produced isn't too loud. However, it has a quicker response time, making it easier to play for fast beats.
- **Jazz:** Much quicker and lighter, and the toms are the same size as those in the fusion set but shallower. The bass drum is also usually smaller, 18-inch by 14-inch.
- **Electronic/Virtual:** These provide an almost never-ending selection of sonic options and have advanced each year. You can choose whatever sound you want and purchase a basic kit up to a fully professional one. They can work with apps and software, and can be a lot of fun.

Hand Drums

Hand drums are almost as common as acoustic sets, and you can play them by hand with a tipper or a mallet. Each has its own technique and pattern.

3. *A Cajon is a Peruvian hand drum. Source: Muchinaespn, CC BY-SA 4.0 <https://creativecommons.org/licenses/by-sa/4.0>, via Wikimedia Commons: https://commons.wikimedia.org/wiki/File:Cajon_Tocador.jpg*

Some popular types include:

- **Cajon:** A box-shaped Peruvian drum, performed using the hand, a drumstick, or a brush, it is frequently utilized in acoustic concerts. While playing the Cajon, you can also sit on it.

- **Bongos:** Afro-Cuban drums that are frequently played alongside congas. One is smaller (macho), and the other is bigger (hembra).

- **Congas:** Are a set of two or three Cuban drums. Small (quinto), middle (tres dos), and big (tumba) sizes are available.

- **Tablas:** Indian drums that are played with the fingers and heel of the hand are called tablas. There are two different kinds: tiny, made of wood (table), and giant, made of metal (dagga).

African Drums

A broad family, some of the more common types are:

- **Udu:** The Udu is a clay-based drum from Nigeria that may have one or two chambers. This can be played by tapping your fingers or the palms of your hand.

- **Talking:** As you squeeze the rope and strike the drum, these drums are positioned beneath your arm. A striker has the ability to change the pitch.

- **Djembe:** A well-liked hand drum, the djembe can have synthetic or goatskin-shaved heads and can be automatically or manually tuned.

Marching Band Drums

These drums are the heart and soul of any marching band. The most popular ones are:

4. *Marching band drums are the heart and soul of any marching band. Source: Shaun C. Williams from USA, CC BY 2.0 <https://creativecommons.org/licenses/by/2.0>, via Wikimedia Commons: https://commons.wikimedia.org/wiki/File:Marching_band_drum_line_(3688027341).jpg*

- **Front Ensemble:** The front ensemble is a set of drums that is stationary. It has many percussion variations, and these include the drum set, vibes, hand drums, xylophone, timpani, marimbas, glock, frame, bass drum, and other instruments.

- **Bass:** Low-pitched and available in several sizes.

- **Marching Snare:** This is not the same as the standard version because it has a Kevlar head so the sound is much deeper.

- **Multi-Tenor:** Available in multiple configurations but usually sets of 4 to 6. They have a higher pitch, and you use mallets or sticks to play them. They may be accompanied by a small accent drum called a shot or spock.

Orchestra Drums

5. *Timpani drums are the orchestra's most recognizable drums. Source: The original uploader was Flamurai at English Wikipedia., CC BY-SA 3.0 <http://creativecommons.org/licenses/by-sa/3.0/>, via Wikimedia Commons: https://commons.wikimedia.org/wiki/File:Standard_timpani_setup.jpg*

Orchestras use multiple drum types to add intensity and dynamics to the music. These include:

- **Timpani:** The orchestra's most recognizable drum is without a doubt the Timpani. Because it is composed of heavy copper, it makes a loud sound that reverberates all around when it is hammered with a mallet. A foot pedal is typically included as well, which helps in sound tuning.

- **Concert Bass:** The concert bass is a percussion instrument that is played standing and struck with a large mallet. They are larger than standard bass drums, with a 40-inch or more diameter.
- **Concert Snare:** Keeps the rhythm throughout the piece with a snappy, short beat. They can also be used for military-style music.

Different Types of Drumsticks

Drumsticks are integral to learning to play, and choosing the right ones isn't always easy. There is an almost overwhelming choice of types to pick from, and you won't have the time or money to try them all. That means you need to understand how to choose the right ones. Before that, let's look at the different types available.

Different Types of Drumsticks

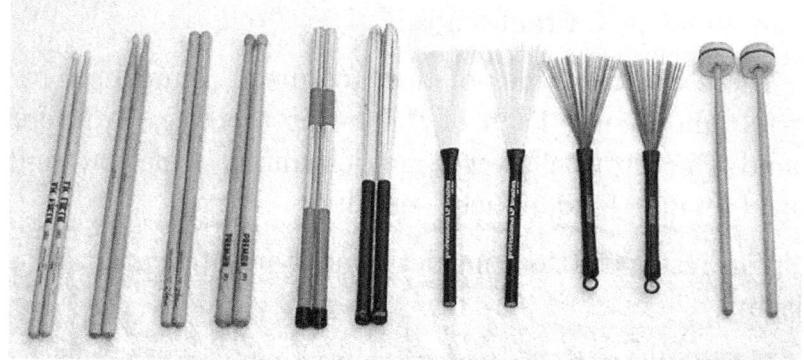

6. *Getting the right drumstick is an essential part of playing the drums. Source: Andrewa, CC BY-SA 3.0 <https://creativecommons.org/licenses/by-sa/3.0>, via Wikimedia Commons: https://commons.wikimedia.org/wiki/File:Drum_sticks.jpg*

As important as choosing the right drum set is, getting the right drumsticks is perhaps more important. You need sticks that allow you to feel comfortable and produce the best possible sound, and you also need them to be well-balanced. There are a lot of variables here, so take a look at those first.

The Tip Shape

Drumsticks have five tip types:

- Acorn
- Barrel
- Oval
- Round or ball-shaped.
- Teardrop

Each type produces its own sound, and they all feel different.

The oval tip provides an extensive sound spectrum, while the teardrop plays focused, warm tones. If you want a bright, clean sound, go for round tips.

There are five types of tips: teardrop, round/ball, oval, barrel, and acorn. Each of those tips produces a different sound. The acorn tip gives you a rich sound, while you want a barrel tip for a loud, punchy sound.

You also need to consider what type of music you are playing.

If you play with an acoustic setup, you want the teardrop sticks. If you need your sound to be heard, go for barrel tips. Beginners should speak with a professional to determine which tips suit them best if they are unsure.

Letters and Numbers

These both represent different things:

- **Letters:** Musical style

- **Numbers:** Diameter of the stick. The lower the number, the bigger the diameter. For example, 8A sticks have a smaller diameter than the 6A sticks. However, as many businesses have not yet implemented their own systems, an 8A stick from a particular company will probably differ from an 8A from another. You should, therefore, experiment with various sticks.

How to Choose the Right Drumsticks:

Here's a step-by-step guide:

Step One: Choose Your Wood Type

First, you must choose the right wood, and drumsticks are usually made of hickory, maple, or Japanese white oak, although laminated birch is now gaining popularity. Each wood type has a different feel, achieved by vibration and flexibility.

- **Hickory:** One of the more common, it is a well-rounded wood type offering flexibility, strength, and impact resistance.

- **Maple:** This is typically lighter than hickory, so you can use larger sticks because they weigh less. It is softer with more flexibility than maple, which means it isn't so durable.

- **Oak:** This is a denser, heavier type of wood that produces more vibration. While oak drumsticks are usually robust, it isn't unheard of for them to break without warning.

- **Laminated Birch:** Made of the highest-quality plywood, these sticks last longer but are somewhat cumbersome.

Step Two: Choose Your Material

Next, you need to choose the material the tip is made from. Typically, they are made of wood, Delrin, or nylon. Wooden tips offer a dark sound on a drum and are not so articulate when used on a cymbal. Delrin is said to be more durable, while nylon tips offer a clean, right sound when used on the cymbals.

Step Three: Choose Your Shape

Tips come in several shapes, each offering a different sound, and each shape is available in several sizes—generally, the bigger the tip, the deeper the sound.

- **Barrel:** Their contact area is wide and smooth, providing a booming, dark sound.
- **Acorn:** Their contact area is the largest, reducing the contact sound significantly and producing a dark, rich sound on the cymbals.
- **Ball:** Their contact area is small, providing a bright contact sound.
- **Oval:** These are somewhere between the ball and barrel tips.

Step Four: Choose Your Thickness

Next, choose the thickness. This is important because different thicknesses produce different sounds. You can determine the thickness in two ways: a model number and an understanding of the diameter.

In terms of the model number, the higher the number, the thinner the drumstick. For example, an 8A is thinner than a 6A. However, this isn't the most reliable way of telling because most companies have their own parameters. So, knowing the diameter is the next way. Here are some guidelines:

- 7A sticks are thinner and lighter, with a better sound on drums and cymbals. They suit play where less volume is needed.

- 5A sticks are a little thicker than 7A and are typically considered the more flexible and most used.

- 5B sticks are powerful, heavier drumsticks usually used by rock and heavy metal drummers.

Step Five: Choose Your Coating

Choosing the lacquer or varnish coating is done by trying different sticks. Hold each one as you would if you were playing, and let it slide through your fingers. You'll know the right one when you feel it.

Step Six: Choose Your Brand

There are plenty of brands to choose from, but they are not all equal. The best advice is to consider the drumsticks used by your favorite artist or whoever you are trying to emulate. Some of the top brands are:

- **Ahead:** The most popular choice for heavy metal drummers because they are larger sticks and more durable.

- **ProMark:** There isn't much choice of tips with this brand, but they do have some great finishes.

- **Vic Firth:** This has the widest range of drumsticks, typically with a light lacquer. Many of their sticks have painted designs.
- **Vater:** Similar to Vic Firth, but they offer more choice of shapes.

Step Seven: Experiment

The only way to choose your drumsticks is to experiment and see what works for you.

Accessories

The final thing to consider is the accessories you might need.

1. **Drummers Multi-Tool.** These are necessary. No matter where you are, something can go wrong that needs fixing, such as a drum out of tune or the bass pedal rattling. Multi-tools contain a drum key, hex keys, screwdrivers, and a wing-nut loosener, at the very least.

2. **Earplugs:** Drums can be extremely loud and seriously harm your ears over time. For long-term use, you should buy a good set of foam plugs, though you can get away with using inexpensive ones in an emergency.

3. **In-Ear Monitors/Headphones:** Most drummers may occasionally jam to music as part of their preparation, so having a good set of in-ear monitors or headphones is essential. Make sure the cable is long enough so you won't become tangled. By doing so, the volume is lowered and you may hear clear feedback.

4. **Drum Dampening:** Drums occasionally need a bit of tweaking to ensure the sound hits the sweet spot, and drum dampening helps you do that. Make sure you buy a decent brand.

5. **Stick Bag:** You should keep track of the various pairs of sticks, brushes, and mallets you will likely collect while playing the drums. The ideal method to keep your sticks and other essentials with you is in a stick bag that has enough space.

6. **Practice Pad:** You won't always be able to play at full volume unless you have a rehearsal space, so be prepared with a practice pad so you can hone your technique, rudiments, and chops wherever you are. Most can be placed on top of a snare drum or on a stand and feature a sturdy base and rubber surface.

7. **Drum Key:** This is one of the most essential accessories you need to help you tune your drums, adjust your pedals, and tighten your memory locks. Make sure you always have at least one with you at all times.

8. **Drum Tuner:** All drummers must be able to tune their drums, and while you should learn to tune by ear, you should at least start with a drum tuner. These give you note measurements or Hz measurements, allowing you to get consistent tension on each rod.

9. **Metronome:** A must-have piece of kit, a metronome can help you learn to keep time and is perfect for those who want to try different tempos. You can choose between a hardware metronome or an app.

10. **Spare Parts:** You should always have a supply of spare wing nuts, cymbal sleeves, cymbal felts, hi-hat felts, snare wire strings, and tension rods as a bare minimum. These are the things that are likely to break or go missing.

Chapter 3: Basic Techniques

Basic techniques are the backbone of your practice, and you'll use them to improve your playing and learn more advanced techniques. This chapter will discuss your drum-playing posture and some basic strokes you must learn, followed by a discussion on adding dynamics to your playing. We'll finish with a dynamics exercise for you to try.

The Right Posture

You might think you only have to sit up straight on your stool to play the drums. You would be wrong. For drummers, ergonomics is relatively easy, but not always. A straight back is only one aspect. How you position your drums will determine the majority of your stance.

7. *Your posture while playing the drums depends on how you position your drums. Source: https://www.pexels.com/photo/man-playing-drum-near-bay-at-day-time-876714/*

It can strain your body and lead to injury if you have to slouch, hunch over your drums, or sit too high or low. A general outline will ensure you're comfortable because everyone's bodies are different.

Throne Positioning

Your throne height determines your posture. For instance, if you are 6 feet 2, you will be higher than a drummer who is 5 feet 4 inches tall.

1. Place your feet firmly on the ground while seated on your throne. Permit your feet to rest naturally.

2. Slightly slant your legs downward. The most comfortable posture appears to be at 90 degrees, but if that doesn't work for you, try a little wider.

3. Adjust your hi-hat and bass drum pedals so that they line up with where your feet are.

Foot Positioning

1. Step on the pedals while being careful not to twist your feet. You don't want your left foot to be too far in or your right foot to be too far out, for instance. You must have effortless access to everything.

2. If you have a backrest, do not lean back on it. Sit up straight. In fact, ignore its presence. Sitting on the edge will give you more control and a better posture.

When you are settled, and in the proper posture, you may start arranging your drum kit around you.

Snare Positioning

Put your snare drum where you would put a steering wheel. It must be placed comfortably and evenly spaced apart from each of your feet.

Place your bass drum and hi-hat next, then arrange the rest of your kit around these three. Once everything is set up, you ought to feel relaxed enough to play for a long time without becoming tired or hurt.

Basic Drumming Strokes

This part will teach you some fundamental drumming strokes, or "rudiments," if you've never played before. Later, we will go over these in further depth.

It's best to learn these from a young age because they make it easier for you to move around your drum set and help you develop proper timing and technique. We'll examine five fundamental principles:

1. Single Stroke Roll

This is the absolute basic stroke and the easiest to learn. Learning this allows you to play many solos, beats, and fills, but it won't be easy to speed it up or start with your non-dominant hand.

8. *Single stroke roll. Source: The original uploader was Brad Halls at English Wikipedia. SVG by Magasjukur2, CC BY-SA 3.0 <https://creativecommons.org/licenses/by-sa/3.0>, via Wikimedia Commons: https://commons.wikimedia.org/wiki/File:1_single_stroke_roll.svg*

Start by learning this on a drum pad, then move to the drum kit when you think you have it.

- Sit before a flat surface and tap it with alternate hands, ensuring you do it evenly and smoothly.
- When you move to a drum pad or drum, repeat, but make sure you start slowly.
- Make sure your drumsticks bounce off the surface. You should never force them down.

While this is the easiest stroke to learn, you should not limit yourself to playing one drum or cymbal at a time. You create a unique sound when you play each hand on a different one.

2. Double Stroke Roll

This stroke also sets you up so you can play the other rudiments, and it helps you learn to use your fingers properly. It is similar to the single stroke, but you play two strokes on each hand this time.

You will likely find the strokes from your non-dominant hand have a weak sound, so spend time focusing on strengthening it so all your strokes are even. You will also find that the second stroke on each hand is weaker. Again, strengthen it by practicing the leading rudiment with each hand.

Switching between drums with the double stroke won't be easy because the toms have a much looser surface tension than the snare or a drum pad. This is an area you must spend time practicing.

3. Single Paradiddle

This is a combination of the single and double strokes, another important stroke to learn. It teaches you how to play a repeating pattern and balance your hands. However, because there are multiple variations, you must learn the single paradiddle before you can even think about any of the others.

9. *Single paradiddle. Source: Fabrizio Leoni, Public domain, via Wikimedia Commons:*
https://commons.wikimedia.org/wiki/File:BATTERIA_Single_Paradiddles_01.jpg

The rudiment requires you to alternate two single strokes between your hands and then return to your starting hand and play a double stroke.

There are many uses for the single paradiddle, allowing you to move accents to create unique grooves and fills. A straight single paradiddle is a great fill, but this really starts to shine when you add dynamics.

4. Flam

This requires you to play one stroke with each hand, but the second comes quickly after the first. The first stroke is known as a grace note and is very light, falling into the second louder, more powerful one. You need to learn these as early as possible because they are included in more difficult rudiments.

To play the flam, raise both arms, one higher than the other. Then, allow them to drop at the same time. While this is considered to be one note, repeating flams can be played to help you learn to alternate your starting hands. They work well as fills, whether alone or in a different pattern.

5. Double Paradiddle

This rudiment adds some fun to the single paradiddle. You use it to create a six-note pattern by adding two extra single strokes at the start.

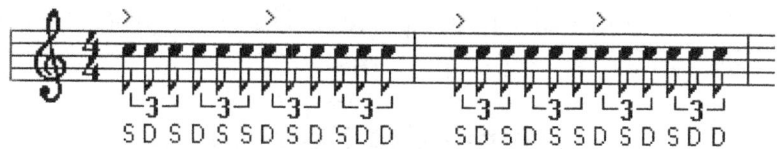

10. Double paradiddle. Source: Fabrizio Leoni, Public domain, via Wikimedia Commons: https://commons.wikimedia.org/wiki/File:BATTERIA_Double_Paradiddles_01.jpg

There are 12 beats to the bar here, so the double paradiddle can be played with a triplet feel.

You can add an accent to each quarter note to give your double more oomph, and in a six-note pattern, you could accent the first and third notes.

These are some of the best for grooving. As the notes are lined up, using your left hand to play a backbeat on the snare is easy. And that backbeat can be kept going when you play fills.

Tips to Practice Rudiments

It can get a little repetitive when you practice rudiments, but repetition is a necessary evil. Here are some ideas to help you keep things interesting:

- Play them over your favorite tunes.
- Practice with a metronome to increase your speed.
- Play all five rudiments one after the other.
- Practice, practice, practice.
- Incorporate them into fills and drum beats.

There is no rush. Slow down, learn your techniques, and practice them until you are perfect. That way, you'll be ready to face more challenging patterns.

Dynamics Exercise

When you control each of your limbs fully, you have all the tools you need to help you play dynamics. This refers to nothing more complicated than how soft or hard you hit the drum and how quietly or loudly you play. The exercise below is designed to help you improve your dynamics and gain independence over your limbs.

First, position yourself comfortably in front of the kit:

- Your left hand will play the snare.
- Your right hand should be on the floor tom.
- Your left foot should be on the hi-hat pedal.
- Your right food should be on the drum bass pedal.

The idea is to hit everything simultaneously, playing at medium volume and steadily.

First, decrease and increase the volume of both legs and arms simultaneously:

1. Increase all four volumes together as you are slowly building them up.
2. When you reach the top volume, slowly decrease it until you reach the quietest volume and your sticks are an inch or less from the drums.
3. Go back up to medium volume. The complete cycle of medium-to-high-to-low-to-medium should take about 30 seconds.
4. Repeat several times and then go to the next part of the exercise.

You will increase and decrease the volume this time, but use one foot or hand at a time. The remaining three limbs must remain at medium volume.

1. Increase the snare volume to its loudest, keeping the other three at medium.
2. Take the volume back down to low, ghost notes.
3. Go back up to medium volume.
4. Repeat for the other three: tom, hi-hat pedal, and the bass. Always keep the other three at medium. Each cycle should take 30 seconds.

You don't even need a drum kit to practice this. Do it anywhere, anytime, by tapping your feet on the ground and your hands on your thighs.

When you are comfortable with this, you can increase the challenge. Using the same exercise:

- Add random ghost notes and heavy accents.
- Decrease and increase using two or three limbs simultaneously.
- Increase one limb's volume while decreasing another.

Now, you can do the same thing with patterns, fills, and drum beats:

- Cycle through the entire decreases and increases for each limb.
- Add soft and hard accents on different limbs, using as many different combinations as you can.
- Increase the volume of one or two while decreasing the others at the same time.

The Benefits of Dynamics

- Depending on your drum kit's volume contrasts, you can learn to play one beat in multiple ways. You can bring out the best parts of a complex pattern or play 4/4 grooves in the correct place. Think about the role each cymbal or drum's volume plays in the song and the feel of the drum.
- Depending on where you use your new fills and how you use them, they will take on a new life.
- Simple patterns can be made to sound interesting and complex.

- Your drum volume can be perfectly blended with other instruments, no matter the situation or drum kit.
- Louder drum sections will pop, while you will bring intimacy to quiet sections. You can bring the audience into the music by working on your dynamics throughout the entire song.

Chapter 4: Rhythm and Timing

Two of the most important parts of any music are rhythm and timing because listeners will not put up with out-of-control, out-of-time music. The only way to learn how to understand rhythm and track time is by counting.

And the easiest way to do it is to count out loud, at least as a beginner. You can learn to count in your head in time, but even advanced players do it, especially when learning a difficult rhythm.

11. Rhythm and timing are a vital part of any music. Source: https://unsplash.com/photos/man-playing-drum-set-on-stage-QdmUva6qBTk?utm_content=creditShareLink&utm_medium=referral&utm_source=unsplash

So, what is counting?

It is how you outline the rhythm and mark the pulse. It's that simple.

The Pulse

The pulse, otherwise known as the meter, is the song's heartbeat. When you listen to music, do you tap your toes? That's the pulse. When you play in 4/4 time, a measure's four beats are counted as 1, 2, 3, 4.

Here's one way you could practice counting a quarter-note pulse:

1,	2,	3,	4,
pear!	pear!	pear!	pear!

1, 2, 3, 4

Practice placing an accent on every beat. As you count, play a note on your drum or tap your thigh:

1, 2, 3, 4, **1**, 2, 3, 4

1, **2**, 3, 4, 1, **2**, 3, 4

1, 2, **3**, 4, 1, 2, **3**, 4

1, 2, 3, **4**, 1, 2, 3, **4**

Play it again, but only play the accented beats and count the others.

Eighth notes

Eighth notes are half the duration and twice as fast as a quarter note. Maintaining the pulse count on the quarter note as above, add a syllable between every beat:

1, and, 2, and, 3, and, 4, and

Now practice adding an accent to each downbeat:

1, and, **2**, and, **3**, and, **4**, and

And then the upbeat:

1, and, **2**, and, **3**, and, **4**, and

Then, as before, practice accenting every beat individually, counting the other notes instead of playing them, and then try them in groups. Choose one upbeat and count each eighth note, but only play that upbeat.

Sixteenth Notes

These notes are counted by keeping the above eighth note count but adding another syllable into the mix:

1, e, and, ah, 2, e, and, ah, 3, e, and, ah, 4, e, and, ah

Accent each number, then the 'ands,' the 'e's,' and the 'ah's' in turn. Make sure each 16th note is accented, and then play it as the only note while counting the others.

While you can use a metronome to help you practice your timing, your ear is your best tool. Record your practice sessions and listen to them. That's the only way to know what you sound like and where you need to improve.

Reading a Drum Score

A drum score is the music or beats it is written for. Many drummers believe they don't need scores as they play by feeling, but you'll struggle if you can't read one. Let's say you get asked to fill in for a drummer, but all you have is their drum scores. If you can't read them, you can't play.

A drum score comprises three main bits:

1. **The Stave**

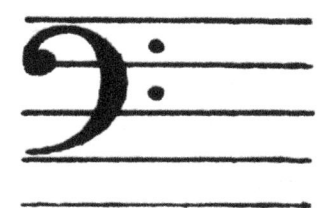

12. Staves are 5 equally spaced lines. Source: Pearson Scott Foresman, Public domain, via Wikimedia Commons: https://commons.wikimedia.org/wiki/File:Staff_(PSF).png

This one is easy, as it's nothing more than 5 lines equally spaced. Also called the staff, this is the base for the notes to rest on. It tells you visually where the note is located, which is much easier than guessing the note's pitch if it's just written on plain paper.

At the end of the stave is a bar line, representing the end of the measure. When you get to the bar line, your count restarts.

1. **The Time Signature** - The book has talked about timing already, and each musical piece has its own. Some pieces change their counting cycle in certain places, and timings may vary depending on the musical interpretation. The time signature tells you the timing to use.

2. **The Notes**

13. A written score must have notes. Source: Ofeky, Attribution, via Wikimedia Commons: https://commons.wikimedia.org/wiki/File:Music_note_A.jpg

Obviously, you can't have a written score without notes. These tell you what type of notes to play and what's coming up.

Let's look at these in more depth.

1. The Time Signature

The time signature helps you interpret the timing. Two numbers are written on the stave, one above the other. The top number tells you how many beats to count, while the bottom number tells you each beat's time value.

4/4 is the most common drumming time signature, which is why it's often called "common time." It's not hard. 4 beats are counted, each a quarter note. When you first hear music, you won't be able to tell the timing unless you are a pro. That's why you need to understand the drum score's time signature.

2. Reading Drum Notations

With most musical instruments, how the notes are positioned on the stave tells you the pitch, but with the drum, the notes or notation tells you which drum to play. Those drums played using drumsticks are higher on the stave than those played with pedals.

3. Reading Music Symbols

You may also spot that drum notes can be in different forms. Each form represents how long the note lasts.

Learning to play the drums is not easy. Not only do you have to teach your mind and body to coordinate differently, but you also have to learn how to read these drum scores. You may be tempted to skip over it and just learn to play by ear, but there are several reasons why you should learn the scores:

- **You'll Find It Easier to Self-Learn.**

Learning to read the drum score will make life easier if you prefer to self-learn the drums. If you don't have a tutor, getting feedback on your playing and technique is almost impossible, which is why online learning uses the drum score to teach you what to play and how fast. You'll also need to use drum scores when learning rudiments, so you need to be able to read it and understand counting.

- **You Can Play Anything.**

Imagine hearing a song that you know would make a killer drum piece. You may attempt to play along by ear, but unless you are a skilled drummer, it is guaranteed you'll only end up frustrated. But what if you could obtain the song's whole drum score?

That drum score gives you everything you need to learn and play along to that song easily.

- **You Can Play with a Band.**

Although musical notations are slightly different for drummers, all musicians understand timing the same way. When you can read a drum score, you can learn to count. This is crucial if you want to play drums with a band. When you can count, any song can be broken down so you can easily play them.

Level up Your Drumming with a Metronome

When you use a metronome to practice timing, it helps your sense of internal time improve. You just need some time, patience, and a metronome – physical or an app – to level up your drumming.

14. A metronome can help you practice timing. Source: https://www.pexels.com/photo/close-up-of-a-moving-metronome-7220729/

1. Practice Your Weak Areas

That is what you should be working on if you feel you are having problems. You can identify your weak points and strengthen them with the aid of a metronome. You may, for instance, loop between three bars of groove and one bar of whatever it is that you find difficult to maintain time with. It will get simpler the more you do it.

2. Speed up by Starting Slow

The majority of drummers use a metronome to practice maintaining a steady tempo while slowing down a challenging bit. By doing this, you may master difficult sections without making mistakes and steadily increase your speed as you advance.

While isolation can be trying at times, it is by far the most effective technique to use. Determine which note value in the challenging section is the shortest, set your metronome to 60 beats per minute, and then play that note value at a speed that equals 60 beats per minute during the entire passage. For instance, you should play the passage so that every sixteenth note gets one beat, every eighth note gets two beats, and so on, if the shortest note in the passage is a sixteenth note. When you feel you've got it down, start accelerating the metronome until you are moving at the desired speed.

3. Use Different Tempos

Practice playing fills and beats at every tempo while varying the click speed. Focus your practice on those tempos since you could find some of them more difficult to play along with. By experimenting with various tempos, you can identify your weak points and take steps to strengthen them.

4. Displace the First Beat

Nothing dictates that the downbeat is the metronome click. Reggae or swing can be played off-beat, and fantastic things can be done. This is only possible if your initial beat does not coincide with the metronome's first beat. Go a little crazy, move everything by a 1/16th note, and enjoy yourself.

5. Practice Your Fills

During a drum fill, every drummer either slows down or speeds up. Rushing your fills when the tempos are slower or speeding them up when they are faster is one of the most common mistakes. When practicing your fills with a metronome, stay within the confines of the groove. Practice sets that consist of four measures with three groove bars or two groove bars plus a fill.

Chapter 5: Exploring Drum Beats and Fills

When you first start to learn the drums, you might ask yourself what beats and fills you should learn. The truth is, there are hundreds of them, but only a few that you truly need to learn as a beginner. These are easy to remember, and the ones talked about below are no more than one bar long and repeated. Once you learn them, you won't forget them.

15. *There are hundreds of beats you can learn to be able to play the drums. Source: https://www.pexels.com/photo/person-playing-drums-1475021/*

Basic Drum Beats for Beginners

1. **2 Kicks and a Snare:** This is the easiest beat, and it was made famous by Queen's "We Will Rock You." It's nothing more than two bass drums and a snare, and you only need one foot and one hand.

2. **Basic Rock:** This is a little more tricky because it includes the hi-hat, but learning it gives you access to many more songs. Make sure you practice playing it at different tempos.

3. **Add a Kick:** This combines the first two, adding kicking drums to give the rock beat some flair. The kick drums and hi-hat notes match one another, making it easy to learn.

4. **Add a Snare:** Add another snare to the rock beat and get a beach-party groove style. This was made popular by The Beach Boys, The Bee Gees, and other similar bands.

5. **The Popular Pop Beat:** You'll hear this in tons of pop songs, and it is not far off the rock beat. The only difference is there is one more kick before the added snare.

6. **Four on the Floor:** Another beat that all drummers must learn. On each bar's four counts, the bass drums must be played.

7. **Hi-Hat 16ths:** If you find it too easy to play 8th notes on the hi-hat, double them. This will require you to learn to play both hands evenly, and when you master it, it can add some intensity to your music.

8. **Cross Sticks:** Certain parts of a song may require you to drum quietly, and that's where the cross stick will

help. Rather than using the tip of your drumsticks to hit the snare squarely, use the shaft instead. This will produce a clicking noise.

9. **Reggae One Drop:** You will only really hear this in reggae music, and it requires the cross stick and bass drum to be strongly accented together.

10. **Disco:** A popular groove that is commonly heard in dance music. It might seem complex, but it will get easier when you learn to lift both legs and drop them simultaneously to play the kick drum and hi-hat.

11. **Slow Blues:** This isn't too different from the rock beat, but there are two hi-hats between the snare and kick drum.

12. **Slow Swing:** Jazz drums are hard to learn, but the basic swing isn't. All you need is the hi-hat and the ride cymbal, and you can add swing to many songs.

13. **Shuffle:** This shares the swing vibe but with a good backbeat. All you need to do is play the swinging pattern steadily and a backbeat on the second and fourth beats.

14. **16ths on the Snare:** Once you learn to play the snare note by itself, this beat is easy and is one you'll hear people practicing in drum shops.

15. **Motown:** the most iconic of them all and possibly the hardest to learn. However, plenty of practice, and you'll soon be playing it along to your favorite Motown tracks.

An Introduction to Drum Fills

Drum fills are nothing but a bridge from one music section to another. They help you show off your personality and shine, creating an atmosphere and drawing attention to what you are playing.

Fills can be as easy or complex as you want them to be. The only rule is that they match what you are playing. Simple fills can give the impression of emotion, liven things up, and excite the audience.

As a beginner, you should learn to play basic fills once you have learned your rudiments. It depends on the drummer's intentions and the song, so there are no strict guidelines about the length of a fill. The majority, nevertheless, range from four to eight beats.

When to Play Drum Fills

When a song switches from one section to another, fills should be played. Drummers should develop the practice of playing brief fills sparingly.

The times a play should be filled are:

1. Adding variation and a smooth transition between verses or sections of a song.

2. To create tension for the following section during a musical intermission.

3. A type of exclamation point, if you will, at the end of a phrase.

4. When a musical work calls for or calls for the addition of a new pattern or rhythm at specific points.

What Is Their Importance?

Learning drum fills can make you feel more confident, and they are a crucial part of your performance, offering the following benefits:

1. They give the beat some character and depth.
2. They allow the drummer to showcase how signature, rhythmically speaking.
3. They bridge two phrases together.
4. They are an outlet for your creativity.
5. They offer drummers an opportunity to play a solo.

How to Get Started with Drum Fills

First, you must master the drumming basics, such as the rudiments, before you can even think about improvising with fills. Once you are comfortable with what you can do, you can start by experimenting with song timings by breaking the timing up using a fill.

One of the easiest ways to start is by learning a beginner fill and playing it over a 4/4 beat every eight measures. As you improve, try changing things up.

So, you need to learn the following first:

- How to read music.
- How to count music.
- How to stick.

The last one means to understand which hand is playing which note. When you can understand this, you can learn the beginner drum fills. To learn sticking, you must understand reading music, and counting. As you can see, it is all one big cycle.

How to Play Drum Fills Faster

Once you can play drum fills confidently, you might want to consider speeding them up and playing for longer. That requires hand and foot strength and good endurance. So, perhaps, instead of asking how to play faster, you should ask how to increase your endurance. Try these tips to help you learn fills and improve your endurance:

Have the Right Mindset

This is not a race, and when you can understand this, you can improve. Time and practice are critical elements, and you cannot learn fills quickly. You need the right mindset, one of growth and patience. Your objectives are simple:

- Practice daily.
- Learn from your mistakes.
- Compare yourself daily to who you were the day before.

Learn Technique

When learning to play the drums, technique is essential, especially if you'd like to play faster. How you hold your sticks is one of the most crucial tactics because it has a big impact on pace.

Hold your sticks firmly so that your arms may move quickly while you play. Pay attention to this. You will become stiff if you use your arms excessively. The same holds true if you use your fingers too much.

The key to a great technique is to concentrate on wrist control. When your wrists are properly aligned, your fingers and arms will follow. Turning your sticks is one of the best ways to improve your wrist control. Some of the top drummers in the world have been observed spinning their sticks. The best approach to learning is to have fun with them.

Learn on a Practice Pad

When you have wrist control, you can start to learn how to increase speed. To practice patterns, use a practice pad or a click track. These pads may be set up in front of you so that you can practice while viewing instructional videos. Repeat this often. The more you practice, the more proficient you'll get and the more endurance you'll gain.

Watch your wrist control once more while you work on it. Finding the highest BPM at which you can play comfortably is the key to increasing speed, after which you should progressively increase the tempo every few minutes.

What Other Methods Can You Use to Learn Fills?

There are plenty of books, videos, and online courses to help you, provided you know how to read music and count. However, be aware that too much theory isn't always a good thing. Not all of it will be solid theory, and some will likely be nothing more than personal opinion. Find a tutor and practice.

Drumming is about more than speed, and most music doesn't require fast drumming. Use a metronome to help you with timing and practice. Have patience and schedule time every day to improve your endurance. Just 20 minutes daily will help you see significant improvements quite quickly.

Remember this: if your drum fills are all over the place, it doesn't matter. You will get better if you put the time and effort in.

Chapter 6: Playing Along to Music

When you practice your newly learned drum-playing skills, one of the best ways to improve is to have a great song to play along to. While this is a great idea and can help you improve, you must practice correctly. It's great fun, but it could all be a waste of time if you don't focus on the right patterns.

Choosing Your Songs

If you have a drum teacher and they ask you to practice some new rhythms, ask for a few examples of songs that contain them. You could let your instructor know your favorite type of music so that they can choose the right rhythms for you. Even better, if they share your musical taste, they'll probably already have some examples of the right songs.

16. *A drum teacher can help you choose what songs to play. Source: https://www.pexels.com/photo/set-of-retro-vinyl-records-on-table-4200745/*

That said, you shouldn't just practice your favorite songs. Keep an open mind and listen to all different musical genres. That way, you won't get bored, and you'll learn a lot more.

Drum Set or Practice Pad?

You need to keep a few things in mind when planning to play along with a song. First, determine if you should use a practice pad or play on a drum set. You can ask your instructor to help you decide. Obviously, you will need access to the drums when you want to practice, and you need somewhere soundproof. If you already have a practice pad at your home, just use that. That said, you must have a drum set handy for a short while every day.

A practice pad is great for learning new rhythms without the distractions of several drums and cymbals. However, you do need to practice on a drum set as well. You can become set in your ways if you use a practice pad too much. Learning a complex rhythm on a pad and then taking it to a full kit is not easy, either, so split your time between the two.

Listening When You Play

You have several options when practicing a song. You might use headphones to hear the song, depending on where you practice. Ideally, have the song volume low so that you can still hear yourself playing, especially if the music is overpowering in places. That way, you can hear everything you need to. You may be tempted to turn up the volume, but if you can't hear yourself, you won't hear if you make a mistake.

That said, if you have a soundproof studio, turn it up and have fun. Practice rhythms and experiment with the force you hit each drum or cymbal, as this can help you learn emphasis on certain rhythmic parts. You'll be interested to hear how different one pattern can sound when played with an emphasis on different drums or music sections.

Rhythm Practice

Mastering a new rhythm pattern is tough if you learn to play it differently from how it is played in a song. However, once you learn the basics, you can play with it, changing emphasis and so on. Hearing one pattern in several ways can stop you from getting bored.

The only way to learn is to go do it. Get some tunes, play along to them, and hear yourself improve as each day and week passes. All the greatest drummers in the world started the same way.

Playing with a Band

When you play in a band, you need more than your individual skills. You need cohesion among all the band members. To ensure you stay in sync with the other players, your focus should be on adaptability, communication, and listening. The remainder of this chapter is dedicated to giving you some tips to help.

Good Listening Skills

1. Pay close attention to the whole band. Listen to them all to understand what they play and how your drums work with the sound.

2. Your attention should be on the rhythm section. You and the bass player should connect well as you both form the groove's foundation. Listen to their notes and patterns to ensure you are in sync with them.

3. Be aware of the band's leading instruments. Pay attention to those playing the melody and the vocals, as these will give you the changes and dynamics in the structure of your music. Adjust your drum playing to support the performance.

Communication Is Key

1. Learn non-verbal cues, typically musical or visual, with the rest of the band. That way, you can communicate important changes to the tempo or transitions.

2. Body language and eye contact with your bandmates are important. These can help you anticipate changes in the music. Gestures, head nods, and other cues can help keep your performance together.

Timing and Tempo Control

1. A good internal sense of timing is crucial, so use a metronome as often as possible to improve your timing and help you stay in sync.

2. Learn to play different tempos. You need to be able to play at different speeds and learn how to transition between song sections. This will make it easier to match the band's pace.

Get to Grips with the Groove

1. Learn to maintain a steady groove and keep it consistent. Add creativity, but don't veer away from the song's foundational rhythm. You need great timing and consistency to keep all the band players together.

2. Listen to the bass. As already said, the drummer and bass player should have a connection, so listen to their notes and patterns to play cohesively.

Learn Dynamics and Song Structures

1. Study and understand how songs are structured. This means understanding the verses and chorus, instrumental breaks, and bridges. Once you understand this, you can maintain the musical flow and anticipate any changes.

2. Pay close attention to the musical dynamics. This means understanding how the intensity and volume changes. You need to practice controlling the dynamics to support the overall sound and enhance the band's music.

Use a Click Track

1. Use a metronome or click track to help you practice while rehearsing. This helps your internal sense of timing develop and helps you learn how to stay in sync with the rest of the group. It also helps you learn to keep your tempo consistent.

Learn to Adapt and Be Adaptable

1. You need to learn responsiveness to cues from your bandmates. That means knowing when changes are coming, such as transitions or tempo changes. Be aware of the band dynamics and adjust your drum playing as needed.

2. Learn to get over your mistakes quickly. They happen, but recovering seamlessly and quickly is a crucial skill to learn. Maintain focus and groove, and you'll have your bandmates' gratitude.

Staying in sync with your bandmates requires listening, communicating, and technical skills. It's not just you, though. The entire band must be cohesive. When you are, you create a strong sound that takes your performances to new levels.

Chapter 7: Mastering Drum Rudiments

Rudiments are the building blocks of your drumming technique. If you don't learn at least some basic ones, you can't play. Perhaps more important is understanding why they are so important.

At their simplest, rudiments are basic drumming patterns players must learn to develop their skills. They are nothing more than a series of strokes played in different combinations, ranging from the simplest single stroke to the most complex. You develop essential skills such as control, speed, precision, and coordination when you learn them. You also learn to control your four limbs independently, teach your body muscle memory, and gain an understanding of rhythm.

17. Rudiments are basic drumming patterns players must learn to develop their skills. Source: https://pixabay.com/photos/drummer-drums-concert-performance-6869168/

Shortly, you will see the benefits, but first, here are some common rudiments you must learn.

Types of Drum Rudiments

You can learn many rudiments, each offering its own challenges and allowing you to learn new ways to express rhythm.

1. **Single Stroke:** These are the most basic, where single strokes are alternated between your hands. These are best to help you develop coordination and accuracy. They include the single paradiddle and single stroke.

2. **Double Stroke:** You achieve a double stroke when you use each hand to quickly play two strokes, including the double paradiddle and double stroke roll. If you want to improve fluidity and speed, this is the way to go.

3. **Multiple Bounce:** Also known as buzz strokes, where a single stroke produces several bounces on the drum. This creates a kind of buzzing noise. They include the triple stroke and multiple bounce rolls.

4. **Drags:** The greatest thing about drags is the diverse sounds you can create when the stick is dragged across the drum. These are made of primary strokes, grace notes, and second grace notes and include the single drag tap and drag ruff. If you want flair in your music, with a little orientation, then mastering the drag is important.

5. **Flams:** These bring grace notes to your patterns, combining them with loud strokes. The commonest rudiments are the accent and tap, which help bring complexity and dynamics to your drumming.

6. **Hybrids:** These are unique, complex patterns comprising different rudiments, and they help you build creativity and learn rhythm. They include the Swiss Army Triplet and Flamadiddle.

The only way to build your skills as a drummer is to learn a wide range of rudiments. Each helps you improve certain areas, such as coordination, technique, etc. Consistent practice is recommended, starting with the singles and working your way up.

Why Practice Rudiments?

Practicing regularly offers plenty of benefits that help you build your skills, including:

Better Coordination, Control, and Hand Speed:

- Regular practice improves hand coordination, helping you learn balanced playing and develop a certain level of ambidexterity.
- It helps you learn stick technique and play consistent strokes.
- It helps you improve your hand speed when you consistently play different patterns at different speeds.

Better Timing and Rhythmic Accuracy:

- Rudiments are exercises in rhythm and help you learn to reproduce complex patterns accurately.
- They improve your timing, allowing you to play at a steady speed and stay in sync with your bandmates.

Improved Technique:

- When you learn the rudiments, you gain access to many techniques, such as drags, ruffs, flams, and more.
- They give you the basis for learning more advanced techniques, such as paradiddles, ghost notes, etc.

Musical Versatility:

- You can apply drum rudiments to many genres, from marching bands and classical to jazz, blues, rock, and pop.
- They improve your versatility and teach you to adapt to different styles confidently.

Encourages Creativity:

- Rudiments are a drummer's language, allowing your creative side to fly free as you develop your own style.

- They give you the tools you need to add accents, dynamics, and rhythm to your drumming.

Boosts Discipline and Mental Focus:

- Learning rudiments requires you to be focused, with discipline and concentration, teaching you to persevere.
- They promote a mind-body connection, which is critical for consistency in your drumming.

Prepare You to Perform with Others:

- Learning to play rudiments prepares you to perform complex patterns confidently.
- They help you learn to work with others to provide cohesion and communication.

Practicing rudiments daily helps you in all those ways and more. It doesn't matter if you are a beginner or you've been playing for a while. They can help you improve your techniques and teach you to play better.

Effective Practice

You must learn to practice effectively to get the best out of learning rudiments. The following tips will help you:

Warm Up:

- Start with a warm-up routine with stretches to get your blood flowing and loosen your muscles.
- Use gentle movements to warm your arms, wrists, and fingers, and do some gentle drumming to prepare for your practice session.

Start Slowly:

- Begin at a slow speed. Your focus should be on accuracy, technique, and playing cleanly.
- When you have mastered it slowly, increase the tempo but focus on precision and control.

Use a Metronome:

- Using a metronome helps you learn timing and how to sync your playing with others.
- Start at a comfortable speed, practicing timing with the clicks.

Consistency and Clean Playing:

- Focus on quality, even strokes, and clarity, and keep your volume consistent.
- Practice with control and intention.

Use Both Hands:

- Balanced drumming comes from using both hands equally, so build this into your practice.
- Start with your non-dominant hand and bring it to the same level as your dominant hand.

Use Rudiments in Your Grooves and Exercises:

- This helps you integrate the rudiments into context with the music.
- Use different variations and combinations to develop complex platters that challenge you.

When you follow these tips, you will find it easier and quicker to learn the rudiments. That said, there is no substitute for consistency and practice. The more you practice, the better you will get.

Hand Speed Drills

These drills are designed to help you strengthen your wrists, hands, and grip while helping you increase speed.

Stretching:

Stretching is one of the most important things you can do right before you play:

1. Stretch your non-dominant arm out before you, palm upward.
2. Use your dominant hand to push your fingers as far back as possible. You should feel stretching in your muscles.
3. Repeat on the other hand and then do both hands again with the palms downward.

Grip Strength:

This helps you control your sticks and play challenging patterns.

1. Choose a tennis ball, stress ball, or something similar.
2. As you watch TV in the evenings, squeeze it as many times as possible.
3. Repeat on each side three times.

Wrist Control:

1. Place a pillow on the table in front of you.
2. Practicing hitting your sticks on it – they must not bounce back.

This helps you learn not to depend on the momentum of your drum's bounce-back.

Finger Coordination:

This helps you use each finger independently and helps you pivot and control your sticks.

1. Set up a metronome.
2. Tap each finger independently for several beats.

Chapter 8: Progressing with Your Drumming

Professional drummers make it all look so easy, but as you are discovering, there is more to drumming than just hitting the drum with a stick. Those professionals have spent a long time practicing their craft.

18. Practice can help you become a professional drummer. Source: https://pixabay.com/photos/drums-set-people-man-concert-2599508/

Here are some tips to help you improve your technique and progress in your drumming:

1. Arrange Lessons

While you can learn some basics without a tutor, you should attend lessons to improve your techniques. There will always be something new to learn, too. You don't have to attend physical sessions. You can use online tutorials to help you.

2. Find the Right Teacher

Choose the best teacher if you decide to seek one out. Select a knowledgeable instructor who can teach you what you need since they will inspire you to keep trying to get better rather than give up.

3. Learn the Rudiments

As the foundation for all of your drumming, you should learn these as soon as possible. A series of more than 40 may be broken down into five key lessons, which were discussed previously in the book.

4. Practice

Practice truly does make perfect. The more you practice your rudiments and techniques, the quicker you will improve.

5. Use a Metronome

One of the most important talents is consistency, and one of the best tools for learning is a metronome. While traditional metronomes have pre-set speeds, utilizing a digital metronome lets you select your tempo and timing. These create musical time and set the speed for you to work to. You can practice your rudiments at the appropriate speed by setting it to 60 BPM. When you feel confident enough, increase it.

The only problem with a metronome is that you can't hear it when you drum. You can purchase clip-on or wearable devices to feel the beat rather than hear it.

6. Learn to Keep Your Feet and Hands Independent

If you watch any experienced drummer, you'll notice one thing: their coordination. When you drum, you use your four limbs, sometimes together, sometimes independently. Probably the biggest challenge you will face is to play your hands and feet independently, depending on the drum pattern. You can practice this with linear exercises.

7. Be Comfortable at Your Drums

The majority of beginners don't consider how their kit should be set up, and most will find it difficult and uncomfortable to play their drums. Every piece of equipment should be accessible without requiring any bending or stretching. The rack toms should be angled toward you, and the snare should be placed just above knee height between your knees. Look at how your favorite players are set up.

8. Have the Correct Posture

The comfort of your drums is only one aspect of the equation. One more is posture. You won't enjoy playing the drums and run the danger of damage if you don't sit properly. The appropriate posture will allow you to play the drums for a long time while remaining relaxed. Making sure your seat is at the optimum height is a part of this. Put the drum pedal at your natural foot posture while slightly sloping your thighs backward to support your lower back and spine. Your legs should be at a 45-degree angle with one another.

9. Hold Your Sticks Properly

For most beginners, the matching grip works. In other words, you hold each stick in the same manner, usually between your thumb and index finger. Hold them loosely and around the stick with the remaining portion of your hand. The ability of the sticks to bounce when you strike the drum is necessary for forceful drumming.

10. Choose the Right Technique for the Bass Drums

Choose between heel-up and heel-down. Heel-up tends to be more comfortable as your leg muscles provide more power.

11. Hit the Center of the Drum

This is a critical skill you must master, and it isn't that easy. Avoid learning complex patterns early on, as this will stop you from learning to hit the center. Make sure you do your basic core exercises to ensure good drumming habits. If you struggle to hit the center, your development will be slow.

12. Learn How to Read Music

Many beginners find this touch because it's like learning a new language, but it is essential. Take your time. If you can't read music, it will slow you down, and you won't be able to communicate with your bandmates.

13. Set Realistic Goals

A lack of motivation is the biggest reason for failure, and motivation comes from having realistic goals. Good goals give you direction and a sense of accomplishment, not to mention motivation when you feel you aren't making any progress.

14. Study Other Drummers

Not just your favorite artists because their level is not attainable when you first start drumming. Study local drummers, go on the internet, find videos of others, and study their techniques. Listen to tips from those who have been where you are now, as they can help you progress faster.

15. An Open Mind Is Crucial

Don't limit yourself to one style or drum. Set yourself some tasks, experiment, and try others. Who knows, you may decide to change the course of your adventure.

16. Master the Basics

You can't possibly expect to learn anything more complicated if you can't grasp the fundamentals. Learning new talents takes time, and you must master the fundamentals before accelerating your pace and volume. Develop strong muscle memory while moving slowly.

Tracking Your Progress

If you don't know how you are doing while practicing, there is no purpose in continuing. Because of this, you should utilize a practice chart to track your development. The ideal one resembles the chart below. However, this is only an illustration, and you should create yours with the strokes and patterns that interest you.

	1	2	3	4	5	6	7	8	9
Single Strokes									

Double Strokes									
Triple Strokes									
Single Paradiddle									
Double Paradiddle									
Triple Paradiddle									
Paradiddle-Diddle									
Swiss Five									
Four Stroke Ruff									
Swiss Ruff									
Four Stroke Roll									
Five Stroke Roll									
Six Stroke Roll									

Seven Stroke Roll								
Eight Stroke Roll								
Nine Stroke Roll								
Ten Stroke Roll								
Flam								
Flam Tap								
Tap Flam								
Flam and Stroke								
Flam Triplet								
Swiss Triplet								
Flam Paradiddle								
Drag								
Drag Tap								
Tap Drag								

Double Drag Tap									
Drap Triplet									
Drag Paradiddle									
Drag Five									
Drag to Swiss Five									
Drag to Paradiddle Five									

Simply place a checkmark in the box beside any rudiment you practice. After a few sessions, you can see where you are going and will know what to practice next.

Conclusion

Well, you've made it to the end of my guide on Drumming for Beginners, and it is hoped that you've learned that learning to play is about more than just hitting a drum with a stick. It's a complex learning process with many facets, requiring dedication, patience, and consistency.

In Chapter 1, you learned the fundamentals of drumming, including their role across different musical genres, setting your goals, and the benefits drumming offers.

Chapter 2 discussed the different types of drums and drumsticks, how to choose the right sticks, and the accessories you might need.

Chapter 3 delved into basic drumming techniques, strokes, and posture, while Chapter 4 taught you how to understand timing, rhythm, and how to read a drum score.

In Chapter 5, you learned about drum beats and fills, while Chapter 6 explored how to play along with music and how to play with a band. In Chapter 7, you learned some of the basic drum rudiments you must learn, and I provided you with some drills to learn how to increase your hand speed.

Lastly, you were provided with some tips on how to progress your drumming.

As you've learned, drumming is not easy, but it's a lot of fun, great exercise, and immensely satisfying.

If you enjoyed this book, could you please leave a review for future readers? It would also help other potential readers.

Above all, get out there and have fun with your drumming journey.

References

16 Tips for Beginner Drummers To Improve Technique. (n.d.). Www.drumcenternh.com. https://www.drumcenternh.com/news/tips-for-beginner-drummers

5 Easy Drum Rudiments For Beginners - Drumeo Beat. (2022, June 24). Free Online Drum Magazine | the Drumeo Beat. https://www.drumeo.com/beat/5-easy-drum-rudiments-for-beginners/

6 Metronome Hacks To Level Up Your Drumming - Drumeo Beat. (2020, August 25). Free Online Drum Magazine | the Drumeo Beat. https://www.drumeo.com/beat/metronome-exercises-for-drummers/

6 Steps to Setting and Accomplishing Your Drumming Goals. (n.d.). Takelessons.com. https://takelessons.com/blog/drumming-goals

Drum Set Dynamics: A Simple and Effective Exercise to Take Control. (n.d.). Drumhead Authority. https://drumheadauthority.com/articles/drum-set-dynamics-simple-effective-exercise/

Free Drum Lesson: Beginner Lesson 3 - Learn How To Play Basic Drum Fills And Licks» DrumsTheWord - Online Video Drum Lessons. (2008, December 13). https://www.drumstheword.com/free-drum-lesson-beginner-lesson-3-learn-how-play-basic-drum-fills-and-licks/

Hand Speed Drills and Exercises For Better Drumming. (n.d.). Custom Bass Drum Heads. https://www.custombassdrumhead.com/hand-speed-drills/

How To Have Good Posture On The Drums. (2018, September 27). Free Online Drum Magazine | the Drumeo Beat. https://www.drumeo.com/beat/good-drumming-posture/

How to Play Drums: The Complete Guide for Beginners. (n.d.). Takelessons.com. https://takelessons.com/blog/how-to-play-drums-the-complete-guide-for-beginners

How to Practice Drums Along With Your Favorite Songs. (n.d.). Takelessons.com. https://takelessons.com/blog/practice-drums-with-favorite-songs

How to read Drum Score - Drumming Basics. (2018, March 18). Www.drummingbasics.com. https://www.drummingbasics.com/how-to-read-drum-score/

Larry. (2016, August 18). 10 must have drummer accessories. T.blog. https://www.thomann.de/blog/en/10-must-drummer-accessories/

Loncaric, D. (2022, August 1). How To Choose The Right Drumsticks. DRUM! Magazine. https://drummagazine.com/how-to-choose-the-right-drumsticks/

Melodics. (n.d.). Introduction to Counting Rhythm (for Drummers – and anyone else learning music!). Melodics. https://melodics.com/blog/index.php/2019/10/10/introduction-to-counting-rhythm-for-drummers-and-anyone-else-learning-music/

R, C. (2023, July 14). How to play drums with a band and stay in sync. All for Turntables. https://allforturntables.com/2023/07/14/how-to-play-drums-with-a-band-and-stay-in-sync/

Respecting the Fundamentals (Part II): Tracking Your Progress. (n.d.). Pipebanddrummer.com. https://pipebanddrummer.com/blogs/pipe-band-drummer/posts/4695181/respecting-the-fundamentals-part-ii-tracking-your-progress

Rudiments in Drums: Mastering the Foundations of Percussion – FuelRocks. (2023, June 26). https://www.fuelrocks.com/rudiments-in-drums-mastering-the-foundations-of-percussion/

The Role of the Drums in Rock, Jazz, Blues & Classical. (2019, October 30). The Music Studio. https://www.themusicstudio.ca/the-role-of-the-drums-in-rock-jazz-blues-classical/

The Ultimate Guide to Different Types of Drums. (2018, November 1). TakeLessons Blog. https://takelessons.com/blog/guide_to_different_types_of_drums_z07

undefined. (2022, May 4). 10 Health Benefits of Drumming: A Quick Guide. Drumcenternh.com; Drum Center of Portsmouth. https://www.drumcenternh.com/news/health-benefits-of-drumming

Made in the USA
Coppell, TX
17 January 2024